the luxury
59 untitled nature catastrophe poems

Darren C. Demaree

GLASS LYRE PRESS

Design & Layout: Steven Asmussen
Cover art: Megan Merchant

Glass Lyre Press, LLC
P.O. Box 2693
Glenview, IL 60025
www.GlassLyrePress.com

the luxury

Contents

we have all left before
within the hooded after-
noons of the ignored red-

birds born away from the roots
pouring in sticky smacked
from the sky by the white ring

that frames terribly worth
as an echo of the light
when the wing flaps will field

you'd think the wild shit
the refusal to unfold
as stranger returning

to the wetted the sever-
ing the river that is
a grave's edge of consumption

would pause the elegy
for human beings it does
nothing except pass time

the distant is distant
only in that there are few
woods to wind up inside

anymore the being crafts
a brief reckoning it
was always going to give

burials but this is
erasure we can't bury
bodies default fire

the years warm the day warms
the foot-soles aren't sin yet place
is infinite we watch

with our thumbs inside water
we had a chance to be
like skipped rocks instead we cried

salt into the fresh streams
called each other witnesses
to a deep new ocean

we are salt the world is

a berry the window is

a word for leveling

nativity inhabits

landscape as part of scene

instead of acts one two three

& here i am giving

my tongue a damn useless roll

instead of tending root

i, too, feel like we should
spare each other the living
death of a world where we

believe the blue path time-rots
& this was already
heaven we chose destroyers

of worlds as gods tongue-kissed
the rotten marrow out of
what need to challenge rain

native to a land free
from plans we are still sleeping
in the buried gardens

of understanding the breath
this world does not come from
our lungs we are terribly

unjustified from mouth
to path the birds are bemused
we are the luxury

what comes mid-air is gift
testament naked of this
world clothes so dry they burned

off in human perception
a box with no nails no
tape no structure a turning

reality a dance
so angry it was seen at
all it erased the stream

we are the free weapons

the natural boil gave

us a seat we didn't

want so we set our fires

everywhere cooked a bloom

that was cool to any touch

counted seeds as our own

used our thumbs to gouge the earth

we are the free weapons

what a delight for this
world to let go of loving
us back to combat this

looking into our own eyes
to decide if rivers
should keep their shallow shale lips

from kissing ours the puff
bond is always the weakest
the bloom paradox limps

i tell you these midair
nights where i can only be
the refusal of bad

passages into a land
that does not need or want
my alien shoes tripping

over abundancy
i am happy to be in
awe of my thick window

the little fish die first
in the creek behind my house
when the teenagers piss

caffeinated alcohol
on the small rock sculptures
my three children leave behind

once the moon starts to strut
if you want to watch a word
become wordless just wait

if i could rest here in
this place tell you every
arrival is something

other than death descending
awkwardly striving with
no zeal to join our other

intention to blanket
the world underneath our good
eye's languid perception

wholeness isn't really
health i was born with two hands
with five fingers on each

but each one wanted something
more than i was holding
they were greed dedication

& my garden suffered
for it i'm down to six now
wholeness isn't really

i like the root working
beneath the soil knowing
everything but saying

nothing other than the bloom
or the deep empty hand
& that work is good work re-

gardless of the hot blue
comb removing the old fight
for us please we cannot

a raspberry cannot lie
in my mouth without the slight
fuzz seducing my tongue

into a violent roll
into my teeth i feel
no shame i never feel shame

the world is red enough
that i see the real problem
is only my deep mouth

the smoke can only drift
slowly to the neighbor's field
& then to their neighbor's

field etcetera nothing
escapes please only love
that which can slowly rot please

death can save us always
until there is no more death
only silent spun noon

sleep is always so near
a mother's mouth yet many
of them still leave berries

in the fox tracks for the wind
to bring them as a breath
i was forty when the first

bunch found me quite hungry
& alone was it my mom
does it matter does it

we never could hold shine

the same way the deep-back woods

could hold anything so

we invented new gods that

we said saved us from dark

we rose up gave new shadows

& all that dirty smoke

we invented mercy as

a gift to give ourselves

if all you have is white
offerings all i can give
you is an open ash-

pit to lay them on to mute
the smoke the smell which will
never yield give me green land

or give me a culture
that doesn't roast the damn world
on another promised

each ask a backward way
each gift a confirmation
of our freedom follow

me to unreasonable
giving be lost here right
here lose your name empty-hand

the landscape close your eyes
regardless the light finds you
what return what return

fields my time fire and

a smile a devotion

atoms atoms all blood

i take my brain to remove

the idea of heaven

& i grow more desperate

to save the burial

lands we all share in that way

i'm home with or without

find your chattering ears
pinch them with raw meat the fox
of this moment looks hard

for unsteady listeners
slow your wrong direction
the blood will fill the canals

reality sloshes
do not lie doubt the fox waits
& the crop can be drowned

our bond exists because
not all songs need to be loud
& you are listening

intently you feel good safe
enough to allow my
whispering right now do not

run the mist is not fog
the heaving is real lie down
help me breathe for the lamb

i think of the naming
first how we choose the letters
the syllables the roll

our tongues had to make to lift
the steam of our lungs up
past our teeth to be roundly

heard as beautiful sounds
we did this for all things now
what will we call the end

i was given a large
amount of money by folks
that gave the government

some of their money so i
bought four thousand dollars
worth of flower seeds to plant

on our two-thirds acre
& now high-schoolers sneak up
have sex there good for them

how much care do we give

to the nest once it's proven

that we cannot fly high

enough to build a heaven

that we imagined real

when we first crashed into this

gathering it holds lifts

the nest the leaves sticky time

wings are born inside it

this good evening will come
& that couldn't be further
from what matters to this

world i can make a feast we
can eat the whole damn house
empty it would be splendid

& we would sleep quite well
starving never starts with empty
bellies we carve we carve

you only ever hear
of the barn when the barn burns
the house when someone must

escape into the night cars
when their motors bark at
the moon poorly half of this

our piss-poor dialogue
with nature is refusing
to join in we chose doors

we are known fully this
world knows us absolutely
the hope we've shown to each

other person is a glow
in the night memory
holds we never told the earth

all this damn destruction
was backed by hope do you think
it will hold on because

why settle for heaven
when a clean river can take
you to a new speech that

depends not on a whole life
made local by a god
a new speech that licks the rocks

of this world right now this
world that is real flowering
i don't know what else is

i know the numbers end
after we do i don't care
i can't sing equations

the same way i can sing bone
& tendon a pivot
in the sand that ruins it

a cloudy day with run
& run more clearly our heels
are beautiful ask tide

the red clusters we shape
extravagance like the fox
won't simply take it when

the light on shore disappears
in tide's final season
we collect berries to take

pictures of the berries
i trust our cheeks swallow what
ignorance says collect

a worn handle means what
i know the touch doesn't dull
every good element

but isn't the most value
found in what cannot be
held by hands even the moon

must carry the dark weight
from our oil the meaning
sinks look a damn clearing

run run run run run run
run run run run run run run
run run run run run run

run run run run run run run
run run run run run run
run run run run run run run

run run run run run run
run run run run run run run
run run run run run run

the wild duck fucks with
no man if there is god they
imbued the wild duck

with nightfall with a death beak
let us give this world back
to the wild duck let them

tame racists recycle
them as retention pond chairs
let them give us order

we know winter windows

all darken motherfuckers

are still using coal here

& may the flood find them first

but we are not done re-

moving revelations from

their poor vernacular

they still think god is coming

stop it's the oceans turn

give me the river's shape
let me be taken bit bit
up into the sky let

me get lost in the rocks lost
into the soil as
it opens up to use me

please let me be of use
please i am surviving this
world i i want it fed

what burns will burn what burns

is the green stem we hold up

when our whole bodies tip

with fire rip with fire

drown cloth in it make us

into atoms again did

you know the first man's name

was atom he rebelled &

a fire idea laughed

not yet not yet not yet
not yet not yet not yet not
yet not yet not yet not

yet not yet not yet not yet
not yet not yet not yet
not yet not yet not yet not

yet not yet not yet not
yet not yet not yet not yet
not yet not yet not yet

it's raining i'm bloodroot
lifted up spilled out floating
in rivers until they

decide to toss me at crow
sounds until then i'm not
needed the same way i was

never needed our loud
feet only good for tripping
the rhythm of this land

i spent all morning crouched
picked blueberries at the farm
my neighbor started ten

miles from the capital
building i cleaned them put
them into cups for children

they ate some masked others
we heard thunder welcomed it
a gift the coming storm

we will only be thought
of for lifting the earth from
the earth potting it cup

by cup stunting the roots with
walls what walls are made good
by smashing a rock face in

to the only open
mouth that matters close your trap
wait for songs don't steal them

those baptisms mirror
a good rain finding bodies
that need to be cooled i

get it's becoming hot here
very hot cold here too
very cold here the water

when it stays water is
always a gift sure shut tight
eyes believe in water

do it this way not one
person will fight you take one
square of land wherever

it might be protect it tend
to it let it be weeds let
it flower let no shoe touch

it the bloom even if
it's dull is still a bloom if
asked nothing can be owned

i want to be common

as a bone-gap a specter

a promise that where there

was never an opening

but now the failure brings

us a new place to be frail

& human actual

beauty a failing place where

this world can re-enter

good lord the wind is dry

there are no songs anymore

we are plaintiff here save

us no we will save ourselves

maybe maybe maybe

how much joy there is in those

maybes an existence

beyond this existence real

heaven us not ending

most smoke is a short chase

like a word with two meanings

we see it we remember

one reality we wave

at the tide of the next

body count most smoke lingers

as a gravesite then runs

to the next big devouring

season no fire blinks

we have been commissioned

all of us that swing words birds

like to catch in their beaks

to recreate the forests

on the page which is made

out of trees while sculptors

turn iron into trees

in parks that were cleared out to

make room damn it all

i can see that it all
is too heavy to bring in
to another world why

do you want another world
where you cannot bring stars
or bad creations with you

light all the time means we
lose our bodies in rivers
that end in a god's mouth

we could shed our bodies
for this lonely dirt patch so
use to the rivers that

when we shoved the city deer
onto the highways fields
went barren out of raw guilt

salt salt salt became spice
we could shed our bodies but
what dirt would bend for us

i am convinced that all
politicians can be now
are small death explainers

that want us to believe that
since we are billions now
we should only burn bodies

like burning the world first
before others get a chance
isn't all they believe

a street cracks before heat
can ever rise the mirror
stays the mirror birds stay

above ground at all times watch
the tunnels the only
sparks you will see catch songs burn

music give an old room
to new vacancy degree
to degree we cook joy

color is the real cup
the human cloak the smoking
forests the smoke the steel

the gray to whitening ash
fucking coal defenders
they are so easy to find

it's all ruins & yet
we aren't ruined one bird sings
flight doesn't mean escape

there is no break in death

& no loud conversation

with heaven this world leaks

onto what table the bright

hard song of fighting to

fight against the end of wood

is exhausting the edge

of humanity only

leads to more edge dammit

maybe having children
was a mistake i can't stop
shaking when i think they

could be the last adults they
could kiss the first tide in
ohio i am thrilled they

are here now with me i
needed them but my needs are
bringing forth the ocean

it's midnight & i cough

the terror is grain-heavy

the river is low now

there is flooding everywhere

there is a ski resort

where there was once a blooming

field the farmers have left

each drowned body says nothing

more than a monument

so the wind is holy

that means we should be going

i tell you this world is

heaven that when this world ends

there will be no more god

to worship do you save us

so the wind is holy

that means we should be going

listen listen longer

let's say this world can't fold
into itself the way it
feels like it's going to

that there will be more ocean
that the world will be salt
mostly will we hate the tears

our children cry will they
bury us all at sea run
to no shade don't forget

About the Author

Darren C. Demaree grew up in Mount Vernon, Ohio. He is a graduate of the College of Wooster, Miami University, and Kent State University. He is the recipient of an Ohio Arts Council Individual Excellence Award, the Louise Bogan Award from Trio House Press, and the Nancy Dew Taylor Award from Emrys Journal. He is the Editor-in-chief of the Best of the Net Anthology and Managing Editor of Ovenbird Poetry. He is currently working in the Columbus Metropolitan Library system, and living in Columbus, Ohio with his wife and children. *the luxury* is his eighteenth full-length poetry collection.

Glass Lyre Press

exceptional works to replenish the spirit

Glass Lyre Press is an independent literary publisher interested in technically accomplished, stylistically distinct, and original work. Glass Lyre seeks diverse writers that possess a dynamic aesthetic and an ability to emotionally and intellectually engage a wide audience of readers.

Glass Lyre's vision is to connect the world through language and art. We hope to expand the scope of poetry and short fiction for the general reader through exceptionally well-written books, which evoke emotion, provide insight, and resonate with the human spirit.

Poetry Collections
Poetry Chapbooks
Select Short & Flash Fiction
Anthologies

www.GlassLyrePress.com

CPSIA information can be obtained
at www.ICGtesting.com
Printed in the USA
BVHW072354180123
656596BV00015B/112